Goethe's Oak

A Holocaust Story

John T. Price

Ice Cube Press, LLC (Est. 1991)
North Liberty, Iowa, USA

Goethe's Oak: A Holocaust Story

First Edition
ISBN: 9781948509602
Library of Congress information on file

Ice Cube Press, LLC (Est. 1991)
North Liberty, Iowa 52317 USA
www.icecubepress.com | steve@icecubepress.com

The paper used in this publication meets the minimum requirements of the American National Standard for Information Sciences—Permanence of Paper for Printed Library Materials, ANSI Z39.48-1992.

Designed by Sara T. Sauers
Manufactured in USA

For my father

. . . if these trees could talk.

—ELIE WIESEL
during his visit to Buchenwald Memorial, 2009

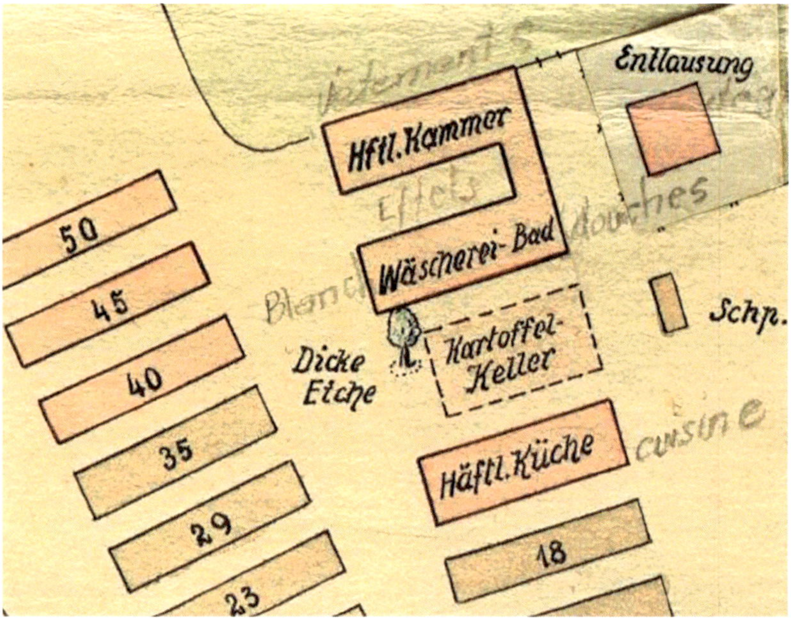
Entlausung
Hftl. Kammer
Effets
douches
Wäscherei-Bad
Schp.
Kartoffel-
Keller
Dicke
Eiche
cuisine
Häftl. Küche
50
45
40
35
29
23
18

Prologue

THIS STORY BEGAN, for me, during a 2015 visit to the Buchenwald Memorial near Weimar, Germany. There, beside tributes to the concentration camp's human victims, I unexpectedly encountered a large tree stump upon which visitors had left hundreds of small stones—a tradition in Jewish culture intended to honor the souls of the dead. Nearby, a small plaque read "Goethe Eiche." Goethe's Oak. As a nature writer and as someone whose life has been profoundly affected by reading, studying, and teaching Holocaust memoirs and by listening to survivors, I wanted to know more about this tree. What special meaning did it hold for Buchenwald's prisoners, and for others, that earned such caring and remembrance?

Goethe's Oak was a centuries-old English oak, *Quercus robur*, that once stood on the north slope of the Ettersberg, a forested *hausberg*, a "home mountain," rising over 1,600 feet above Weimar—Germany's famed city of music, art, and literature. Johann Wolfgang von Goethe, Friedrich von Schiller, and Johann Sebastian Bach were among the luminaries who once resided there. English oaks are native to northern Europe, and some have lived more than a thousand years. Indeed, for generations this massive oak was well known to those walking the ancient trails of the Ettersberg, who rested in its shade and enjoyed the beautiful views.

When the Nazis cleared the forest in 1937 to build Buchenwald (meaning "beech forest"), they spared the oak because of its great size and legendary status, a living symbol of what they considered to be Germany's superior strength and culture—in fact, the image of oak leaves decorated their highest military honor, the Iron Cross. Among the prisoners, however, the tree took on quite a different meaning. Many had undoubtedly heard the story, told for generations in Weimar and well beyond, that in 1776 the renowned Weimar poet and scientist, Johann Wolfgang von Goethe, sat beneath that same oak's branches to write his famous poem, "Wanderer's Nightsong," about his unrequited love for Charlotte von Stein, whom he used to meet there. It is signed "At the slope of the Ettersberg, on 12 Feb. 76." I have included that imagined moment of Goethe's inspiration in this story, along with the poignant verses of the poem itself, as translated by Henry Wadsworth Longfellow. Some prisoners would have associated this poem, as well, with the melodic strains of Franz Schubert, who set it to music in 1815.

Goethe's Oak was the lone tree on the main grounds of Buchenwald, where numerous Jewish, Sinti and Roma, POW, and LGBTQ peoples along with religious and political resisters were imprisoned from 1937 to 1945. There were many children and teenagers in the camp, including a young Elie Wiesel and his father, who died there in 1945. More than 56,000 people perished at Buchenwald. In the midst of their extreme suffering, Goethe's Oak, as stated in the account of the tree at the Buchenwald Memorial, embodied for some prisoners "a legend, a bit of unharmed nature, a reminiscence of the world outside the camp." We can only imagine the details of these reminiscences, but it seems likely they would have included past scenes with family and friends and solitary walks in natural beauty. Perhaps reminiscences, as well, amplified by Goethe's poem, of romantic love and longing.

For writer Ernst Wiechert, imprisoned at Buchenwald in 1938, the tree and its poetic associations were a reminder of the higher principles that human beings might still be faithful to. In his autobiographical novel, *Forest of the Dead*, published in 1945, he wrote:

> It took only a minute to reach the oak which was said to have once cast its shadow over Goethe and Charlotte von Stein. It stood next to a camp road, the only place from which one could now see far out into the countryside. The moon was hanging above the wooded hills, and the last sounds of camp life were gradually subsiding. . . . He looked down for a little while, as much alone as if he were the last man on earth. He tried to recollect all of the verses he had once known, by him who, perhaps, had stood upon this very spot some hundred and fifty years before. Nothing at all was lost of that great life, and even if at fifty years they had fettered him to a galley, nothing would have been lost. "Noble, helpful, and good." Oh no, not even that was lost as long as but a single man could say it to himself and try to preserve it and carry it to his last hour.

Such fragile hopes and reminiscences, however, must have also burdened many prisoners with a devastating sense of loss. For those facing the unspeakable loneliness of their death at Buchenwald, with no hope of escape, what might this tree have offered? Perhaps only a sense, like a thread of light through a forest canopy, of shared belonging to the larger earth, with all its beauty and its pain and its ever-renewing cycles of life and death. Such seems to have been the case for a dying woman and a different tree at another concentration camp, as recalled by witness and fellow prisoner Viktor Frankl in his book, *Man's Search for Meaning*:

> Pointing through the window of the hut, she said, "This tree here is the only friend I have in my loneliness." Through that window she could see just one branch of a chestnut tree, and on the branch were two blossoms. "I often talk to this tree," she said to me. I was startled and didn't quite know how to take her words. Was she delirious? Did she have occasional hallucinations? Anxiously I asked her if the tree replied. "Yes." What did it say to her? She answered, "It said to me, 'I am here—I am here—I am life, eternal life.'"

Tragically, Goethe's Oak was also, at times, a site of torture; victims were bound to it for extended periods. It thus became, for some, a symbol of Nazi brutality. Whatever meaning individual prisoners gave the oak, the tree itself undeniably shared in their suffering—a fact that, on its own, might have evoked compassion and identification among the prisoners. Conditions on the grounds—including the compression of the oak's roots and the lack of other plant life to help the soil retain water and reduce exposure—soon did the tree irreparable harm. Possibly as early as 1942, the oak was in the advanced stages of dying, and there remain no known photos of it in full foliage. There is, however, a small drawing of the tree with leaves, labeled *Dicke Eiche* or "thick oak," on a German camp map from 1941–42.

During an Allied bombing in August 1944 of a nearby munitions factory, Goethe's Oak was severely damaged by an errant bomb and (it is said) burned through the night. Although there were casualties at the destroyed munitions factory, where many prisoners were forced to labor, there were no human deaths from the accidental bombing of the camp itself. The oak alone was hit. Is it possible that the tree's diminished, yet still substantial, branches and trunk prevented others from being injured or killed by the explosion? What is certain is that Goethe's Oak became yet another victim of Nazi brutality at Buchenwald. What remained of the tree's decimated body was felled by the order of camp commanders in the spring of 1945, shortly before General Patton's Third Army, Sixth Armored Division, liberated Buchenwald on April 4 of that year.

The oak nevertheless lives on in the memories of the survivors and in their drawings and engravings, which are on display in the Buchenwald Memorial. This includes the image of a human face, a death mask, which writer Bruno Apitz secretly carved into a piece of wood from Goethe's Oak while imprisoned at the camp in 1944. *The Last Face* is a powerful work of commemoration, directly linking the suffering and dignity of one body, one species, with another. The tree is remembered, as well, by those visiting the Buchenwald Memorial who have reverently placed stones on its preserved stump. I was one of those visitors.

Writing from the perspective of Goethe's Oak—or any nonhuman being—involves taking significant liberties. I have tried to do so with careful and respectful consideration. Part of that effort included learning more about recent scientific inquiries into the social lives of trees. At the forefront of that research is Suzanne Simard, professor of forest ecology at the University of British Columbia and author of *Finding the Mother Tree: Discovering the Wisdom of the Forest.* Professor Simard and others have determined that, far from being isolated, trees are connected to one another through vast underground networks of the symbiotic fungi known as mycorrhizae.

These intertwining fungal rivers—which I refer to in the story as "living words"—supply nutrients and water between trees but also communicate warnings that trigger innate biological defenses. Although, like some humans, there are tree species that send out unfriendly, even toxic chemicals to discourage encroachment on their resources—portrayed in this story as "those who did not wish to connect, to share"—most feed and protect one another regardless of species. This is especially evident when they are dying, when they pass along what remains of their essential nutrients as well as a kind of biological wisdom through these mycorrhizal networks to help vulnerable saplings survive, even those that aren't direct offspring. Their final gift to future generations. As Professor Simard writes:

> When mother trees—the majestic hubs at the center of forest communication, protection, and sentience—die, they pass their wisdom to their kind, generation after generation, sharing the knowledge of what helps and what harms, who is friend or foe, and how to adapt and survive in an ever-changing landscape. It's what all parents do.

What Professor Simard refers to as a mother tree is often the largest and oldest tree in a particular area of a forest, a tree that plays an essential role in that ecosystem's extensive system of interdependency. Although I refer to the mother tree in this story as the female

One, oaks are not biologically gendered; each has both male and female flowers. This ancient being, like any good parent or guardian, is most capable of nurturing and protecting newer generations of trees. Foresters are learning to identify and preserve such trees for the benefit of the surrounding forest, the ecological health of which noticeably diminishes in their absence. This includes, as well, the oak's capacity to feed and otherwise sustain countless multitudes of other species—among them a diversity of insects, birds, and both small and large mammals. It is, quite literally, a tree of life. In his book, *The Nature of Oaks: The Rich Ecology of Our Most Essential Native Trees*, Douglas Tallamy, professor of entomology and wildlife biology at the University of Delaware, refers to oaks as "top life-support trees" and states: "No other tree genus supports so much life."

This research informed many of the characteristics I attributed to Goethe's Oak, likely itself a mother tree, including sensitivity to physical interactions with humans and other creatures. Although it is unclear in what ways a tree might perceive the presence of a human being—through physical touch or chemical signals such as sweat or breath or tears—such awareness is a very real possibility. Less certain is how long and in what form remnants of mycorrhizal fungi that once connected a mother tree to her offspring remain after her death. Do trees retain some other kind of lasting biological "memory" of a parent? Whatever science determines, as someone who recently lost a parent, I choose to believe that such memory does exist within trees, as it does within other sentient beings. As it does within me.

Although the main character of my story is not human, the meaning of its life was enriched by the many emotions and memories that humans attached to it during its years in the camp. Enriched, as well, by Goethe's poem—a testament to the ways that art has the power to deepen, sometimes unintentionally, our connection to nature and to each other. Reminding us of our humanity and sustaining us during extremely difficult times.

By remembering and reimagining the life of this single extraordinary tree, I seek to honor the millions of people who suffered and died at Buchenwald and elsewhere during the Holocaust. I also wish to acknowledge the countless and largely untold losses sustained by nonhuman beings. Suffering does not recognize boundaries among the living during wartime—if it ever does. We are fortunate that Holocaust survivors gave witness to their experiences, and to those of others, in the hope that they might never be repeated. These heroes left, often at great cost to themselves and their loved ones, an invaluable gift to future generations.

Unfortunately, other life-forms did not leave us such words of witness, at least not in any language we can readily understand. As Elie Wiesel observed in 2009, while visiting Buchenwald, where he had been imprisoned as a teenager, with President Barack Obama and Chancellor Angela Merkel: "if these trees could talk." In seeking to give voice to Goethe's Oak, I have only my own limited knowledge, language, and imagination to rely upon. I have tried, nonetheless, to honor the spirit of this being who lessened, even for a moment or two, perhaps beyond any conscious awareness—as nature so often does—the loneliness and suffering of so many.

May we always be inspired to do the same.

Goethe's Oak

LIFE BEGINS WITH a stirring inside. An unfamiliar longing. To grow, to change. To become whatever you are meant to be. In the time and place you are given. For me, that place was an ancient forest on a mountain called Ettersberg. My home there, in this beginning, was an elemental darkness. But I sensed the light beyond. I sensed, too, a mysterious giving. From where it flowed I did not know. Only that it was there and it was good and it was not me.

Not yet.

I felt the sky before I ever knew it. The light, the warmth. The immensity I was born to reach. But first, and always, I had to reach within and down, toward the source of giving. Others were there. I was not alone. They surrounded me, providing, helping, guiding. Especially she who created me. The One. I felt her presence most of all. She told me, in her own way, that this place in the dark was my first and my final home. That it would always hold and sustain me. Here, among the many of our kind. You must never let go of this home. Never forget.

But I was young and impatient to grow. I broke through the surface. The light, overwhelming at first, became gentle warmth. The stirring of life continued. New parts of me were born. Each drop of light settled, like dew, on my first leaves and I drank it in. I wanted more. But others stood between me and the greater light, the sun. I did not understand that they were protecting me from the high, cold winds, from the heat, striving to give me what the sun provides. I wanted only what they had. The One was still there, in the depths below, the sky above. Her giving was stronger because I was part of her. She would help me reach the sky, the clouds. She would never leave me. I sensed this promise from her.

With each new season, I was becoming what I was meant to be. Some would call me an oak, but we are not what we are called. We are not the words others use to name us. We are ourselves, never fully known, even to us—like the sky above, the depths below. There is always more. More to become. We may think we know what we were before, in the beginning, but can we really know? When did this being-ness begin? Perhaps in a long-ago moment, rooted among the stars.

I grew and deepened, more aware of others like me. Some far, some very near. Even the One, whose branches I could now touch. She was still providing, teaching. I learned from her how to listen to many voices. Kin and not kin. Oak and not oak. The forest. The words of the forest are alive, a river of meaning and care. Yes, there were those of our kind who did not wish to connect, to share. Those who, with different words, sought to keep others away. To hurt. It is the way of things. But there were so many of us then, so many kinds of giving, that the hurt did not really matter. We were together.

I became aware of different beings wandering my branches. Sleeping against my body. Raising young amid my flowers. They moved and sent ripples through my roots and leaves, jumping, flying. From her limbs to mine, and back again. In my own way, I could hear their songs. Another kind of living word. When they pressed against me, I could feel their warmth, as if they were smaller suns. Sometimes, their touch was rough—clawing, scraping, leaving scars. But none was so deep that it could not be softened into what I was becoming: part of this world, which was very full. I was full.

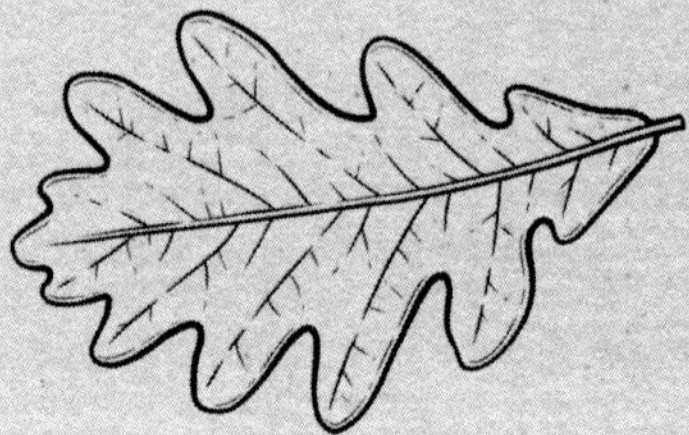

The living words of the forest also sent warnings to call forth inner defenses. Against the dry times, the wet times, the sick times. As the old ones diminished, they gave all they possessed to those who remained that we might live on. But there was no warning the night of the storm. The sky stabbed with fire and there was a torrent of water, too much. Winds bent what should not be bent. There was a breaking nearby, and the earth shook. A scream of living words. The One! Morning brought a shock of light, of heat. She was still there, somehow, giving herself over in the way of our kind. But she was no longer above me. I could no longer touch her branches. There was nothing, now, between me and an empty sky.

Many seasons passed. What remained of the One, her living words, slipped into silence. But I lived on, still becoming. I had no choice. My branches reached toward the clouds, decorated with leaves and flowers, becoming seeds. They fell like rain from my body, upon the earth. Some were carried away, lost forever. Others remained and, in the depths, I sensed new life stirring, new voices. They called to me. I gathered all I could from the sun above and the hidden waters below, giving it over to them. As she had done for me. This giving was difficult, in the dry times, the wet times, the sick times, but there was no choice. They were part of me. Part of what I had now become—provider, protector. Maker of the living words. Maker of the forest.

Another kind of being, not of the forest, visited us more often. Each walked lightly above our roots, but they could also bring thunder and suffering. We knew when they had taken one of our own. We felt each one fall, its pain, its final giving. But some of these beings sat beneath my branches and did not take. The warmth of their bodies against mine, though I was armored against fire, could still be felt. Their songs heard. And it was good. Especially on cool nights, under the moonlight, when they lay beside me, alone or with others. Before the vastness beyond the Ettersberg.

During such a night, near spring awakening, one of these beings lingered and leaned against me. The air was still cold, my leaves not yet born. Even so, I sheltered him from the north wind. I drank the water of his tears. Upon a dry leaf, he made his own living words, speaking them aloud to the darkness:

Thou that from the heavens art,
Every pain and sorrow stillest,
And the doubly wretched heart
Doubly with refreshment fillest,
I am weary with contending!
Why this rapture and unrest?
Peace descending
Come ah, come into my breast!

It was less than a moment in my long life, this visit, this wanderer's nightsong. It did not feel different, just the warmth of another being sitting or sleeping or dying beneath my limbs. So many. But like a seed, it would become something more.

Many more seasons passed. I was now the tallest, the widest, the oldest in the forest. Seedlings from my first acorns had grown and thrived and made acorns of their own. Generations! I gave to them and took pleasure in their giving to others. I offered all my wisdom. Nurtured and protected them, catching winter winds in my branches, softening the summer sun with my leaves. My roots, now vast, kept the soil wet and at home so the forest might thrive. In the high air, I sensed many strange changes in the world, but I stayed true to what I had become. I was now the promise. The One.

Too late, the warning came that day—a flood of living words! Beings were moving everywhere, flying, trampling. Poison clouds of smoke! The ground shook from falling kin—like a river of fire, their pain entered my body. So many! They were falling, dying, trying now to give all they had left, in the way of our kind, but there was no time. I had to save them! I am the promise. The One. But the soil had become like stone, suffocating the living words, the knowing, the helping. I could not reach them. My own! An explosion of light, of sky. Then nothing.

I awoke as if from a long sleep. It might have been spring, but the songs of those who greet the season had become whispers. I reached out for them. The living words were smothered in the flattened earth, the crushed stone. No branches touched mine. No life stirred from up high. I sensed nearby beings, but they were not of the forest. There was no forest. This was another place. Dead structures had been built beside me, where saplings once grew, throwing the sun hard against my body. This heat was new and unbearable. I was thirsty. I sensed that this thirst would never end. I wanted to sleep again, among my own kind. Awaken in that other spring. In the Ettersberg of old.

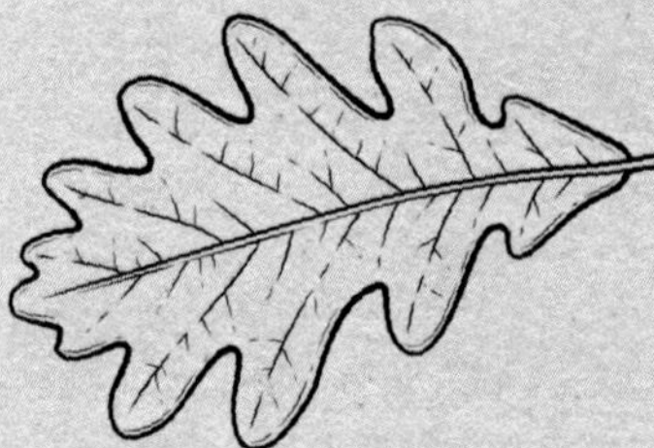

But sleep was impossible. I was what I was. So I brought forth my flowers and leaves, as I had done every spring. I decorated the clouds. There came welcome movements among my branches, the stirrings of life. Below, larger beings drew near, familiar bodies leaning their warmth against my bark. I recognized their steps, their songs, though they seemed of no more substance than the little ones moving among my branches. Unlike some of their kind, they did no harm. At times they even watered me, though it was not enough to cure my thirst. Yet, there was meaning in it. Messages. Like me, they were hurting. They were thirsty. They gathered beneath my leaves, as others once did, sheltering from the sun, the rain, the cold north wind.

There came a day when one of these beings was bound to my body, as others had been. The binding cut deep into my flesh, sharpening the thirst, the pain. The body against mine shook, bent in ways it should not be bent. Tears fell onto my exposed roots and I drank them in. They became part of me. After nightfall, one of these beings returned, alone, touching my wounds from the endless binding. The moon hung above the great open, a breeze caressed my leaves. The being slid deeper into the shadow of my body, trembling, pressing their warmth close to me. I felt their breath upon my bark, heard their whispered song, their living words: *Thou that from the heavens art, Every pain and sorrow stillest.* And then it seemed, without choosing, there came from inside me another kind of giving, different from any I had known. An invisible sustenance, a comfort. A promise: you are not alone.

Across a few seasons more, the beings kept drawing near—for shade, for warmth. And for something else. They sang aloud the living words, in different voices: *the doubly wretched heart… I am weary with contending!* Some words were not sung aloud, though they were just as alive. Silent echoes of what makes a spirit breathe or mourn—tears, unforced, born as naturally as rain is born. *Why this rapture and unrest?* Echoes of what we are or should be. A gentle touch, a promise. *Peace descending.* Of those once loved, now beyond reach; the longing to be near them again, one with them again. Bodies entwined, in joy, beneath this same jeweled light. Breezes dancing in the leaves. Countless nightsongs. *Come ah, come into my breast!* All this, and more, I was giving over to them, without trying. Stirring what remains of the life within. Even in this place of death.

There came a time, one spring, when I sensed that I was finally dying. I desired, in this knowing, to give all that I had to those who might live on. What was left to give? I did not know, but there was no choice. I was what I was. With my remaining strength, I summoned them: the leaves. They would be my last, fewer than before, but the most beautiful I had ever made. They reached higher than ever, caressing the light of the sun. Little ones moved again among the green. New lives. New songs. The beings gathered below, as always, in my shade. To rest, to cry. To sing. I hung on to these leaves for as long as I could. Too early, they fell. The beings gathered my leaves and tossed them to the wind, which carried them over the fence and beyond. When the wind turned cold, they once more pressed their bodies against mine. It was the last I felt of them, this warmth, before drifting into sleep.

Thunder awakened me, unlike any I had known. Harder, closer to my roots. I had, it seemed, grown nearer the earth, though my body still reached high into the night sky. More thunder, a mighty shaking—hot wind and heavy things fell against me. Beings hurried past, fleeing, falling. Saplings in need of protection from the storm! So that is what I did, protect them. Not by choice, but by being who I was. Something immense struck my branches, my trunk. It struck me and not them. There was a great heat and a breaking, and much of what remained of me above fell beside what remained of me below. I sensed I was once again becoming, body burning through the night and into the quiet chill of the morning. A few beings gathered near me. Near this new and diminishing warmth. It was, I thought, my final giving to them.

Spring arrived, but not for me. No flowers, no leaves. No sky. I was far below the surface when I awakened in the dark, the cold. Alone. Afraid. Then, from the depths, like a hidden wellspring, came a murmur, very faint. As when life first stirred within me. Could it be? It was only a trickle of her living words, but it was enough for me to know. The One. She had never left me. She had kept her promise. And so had I, becoming, like her, what I was meant to become. Doing what I was meant to do. In the given place and time. Now, at last, I had returned to where she and the others had always been, even in sleep. The forest. Home.

Do you think this is all there is?

No. There is always more to become. This time, for me, inside those who had drawn near in this place of death and, like autumn leaves, made their way beyond the fence. They would not let me disappear entirely—the being who had lifted their eyes, drank their tears. Helped them live. *You must never let go. Never forget. Peace descending.* Upon my remnant body, they have placed stones that are like acorns. Seeds. From them, something beautiful has grown, and is still becoming. Here and elsewhere. Inside all those who hold to the earth yet reach for the light. All who shelter and comfort others, softening their scars. All who defy the merciless, the cruel, challenging names and the so called inevitable. All who suffer that even a few might be saved. All who love far into the depths, know loss, yet love again . . . and again. All who remember and become the living words. The promise kept. The One.

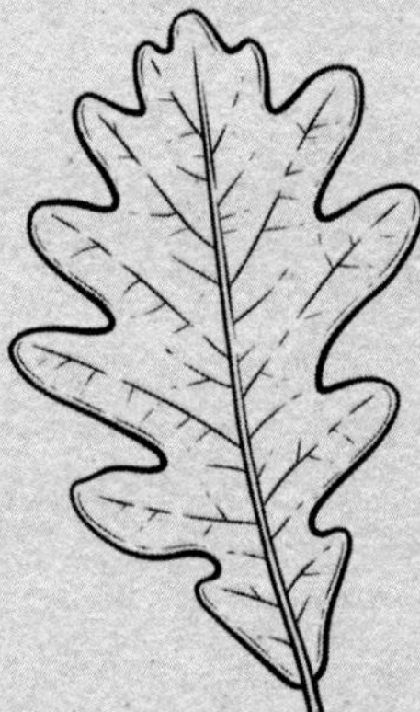

For us, such giving is not always a choice. Sometimes, it is just being what we are. What we are meant to be.

Leaves among the clouds. Roots among the stars.

ABOVE: *Buchenwald Memorial. Goethe's Oak, 1943.*

BELOW: *The preserved stump of Goethe's Oak, with hundreds of memorial stones upon it.*

Acknowledgments

FIRST AND FOREMOST, this book is dedicated to all those who suffered and died at Buchenwald Concentration Camp, as well as their loved ones and descendants. It is also dedicated to the countless and largely voiceless nonhuman victims of war. May their stories continue to be told.

I owe an immense debt of gratitude to the staff at the Buchenwald Memorial Foundation in Weimar, Germany, who were so helpful during my visit in 2015. I'm especially grateful to Dr. Harry Stein, history curator at the Buchenwald Memorial, who graciously responded to my numerous questions about Goethe's Oak, providing a wealth of information and photographs. This book would not have been possible without their collective kindness and generosity. Most of all, I want to thank them for their ongoing efforts to preserve the site of the camp, educate visitors (like me), and keep alive the memory of those who perished there. I encourage readers to visit the Buchenwald Memorial website for more information including ways to contribute to this essential work: https://www.buchenwald.de/en/.

Thank you to the amazing Steve Semken and Holly Carver for believing in this story and offering their incomparable gifts as editors, as well as their creative vision and unwavering support. I've long admired Ice Cube Press, with its emphasis on social and environmental justice, and feel honored to be published there. My thanks to Sara T. Sauers for her inspiring book design and to Ezra Edgerton for the beautiful cover painting. Joanne Wyckoff provided essential advice and encouragement during the early stages of the manuscript as well as steadfast support of my writing for many years—thank you! I'm grateful, as well, for *Orion Magazine*, in whose pages I first wrote about Goethe's Oak.

My understanding of the science of tree communication and behavior relied heavily on the pioneering research completed by Suzanne Simard, professor of forest ecology at the University of British Columbia and author of *Finding the Mother Tree: Discovering the Wisdom of the Forest* (Knopf, 2021). Of oak trees, in particular, I learned multitudes from the work of Douglas Tallamy, professor of entomology and wildlife biology at the University of Delaware and author of *The Nature of Oaks: The Rich Ecology of Our Most Essential Native Trees* (Timber Press, 2021). Peter Wohlleben's *The Hidden Life of Trees: What They Feel, How They Communicate* (Greystone Books, 2016) inspired me, early on, to reconsider my limited preconceptions about tree intelligence. I am grateful to all of them.

Many people offered vital assistance, information, insights, and, in numerous cases, their emotional support as friends during the writing of this book. These include Dave Boocker, Dan Boster, Michael Branch, Simmons Buntin, Pauline Drobney, Hope Edelman, Tom Montgomery Fate, Mark Gilbert, Kristin Girten, Barbi Hayes, Cait Irwin, Jody Keisner, Doug and Yvette Kinney, Jeff Lacey, Elmar Lueth, Matthew Marx, John McKenna, Michele Morano, Steve Newman, David Peterson, Jack Phillips, Todd Robinson, Kyle Simonsen, Abby Spilka, Mary Swander, James Vnuk, and LaReesa Wolfenbarger. At the University of Nebraska at Omaha, my thanks go to Craig Finlay at the Criss Library, my colleagues in the English Department, and my students, who continue to inspire me. Thanks as well to the UNO Leonard and Shirley Goldstein Center for Human Rights, to Mark Celinscak, executive director of UNO's Sam and Frances Fried Holocaust and Genocide Academy, and to Ari Kohen, director of the Norman and Bernice Harris Center for Judaic Studies at the University of Nebraska–Lincoln. I hold a deep appreciation for Samuel

Bak, whose paintings bear witness to the ongoing need for personal, artistic responses to the Holocaust and other human rights injustices. More information on his work can be found here: https://www.unomaha.edu/samuel-bak-museum-the-learning-center/index.php.

The seeds of this book were planted many years ago when I was an undergraduate student in the Department of Religious Studies at the University of Iowa, where Professor Jay Holstein first introduced me to the history of the Holocaust and its literature. Most influential was Primo Levi's memoir *Survival in Auschwitz,* which helped inspire me to become a nonfiction writer and a teacher of the literature of witness. As graduate teaching assistants at Iowa in 1990, Hope Edelman and I had the honor of hosting Linda Fishman, who was born in Poland and lost her entire family in the Holocaust. Linda lived in Des Moines, but she generously traveled to Iowa City to share her life story and memories of the camps. (Her husband was imprisoned at Buchenwald.) Before parting, Linda encouraged me to continue sharing, as a writer and a teacher, the stories of those who experienced the Holocaust. I have done my best to live up to that promise. Linda passed away in 2010, but her story can be heard in interviews for the U.S. Holocaust Memorial Museum and in the book *I Survived Hitler: The Story of Linda Ryngermacher Fishman* by Claudia Holmes.

Finally, I'd like to thank my family. My loving parents, Tom and Sondra Price, demonstrated early on the importance of dedicating whatever talents we have to helping those in need and trying to make this a better, more just world. Their example has been a guiding light. Thank you to my dear sisters, Carrie Anne, Susan, and Allyson, and their families—our bonds of affection only grow stronger. I would be lost without the love and support of my wife, Stephanie, and our sons, Benjamin, Spencer, and Alden, to whom I owe everything. This book, this life, would not be possible without them.

About the Author

JOHN T. PRICE is the author of four creative nonfiction books: *Not Just Any Land: A Personal and Literary Journey into the American Grasslands*, *Man Killed by Pheasant and Other Kinships*, *Daddy Long Legs: The Natural Education of a Father*, and *All Is Leaf: Essays and Transformations*. He is also the editor of *The Tallgrass Prairie Reader*, the first nature writing anthology dedicated to North America's most endangered ecosystem. Born and raised in Fort Dodge, Iowa, he earned his BA in Religion, MFA in Nonfiction Writing, and PhD in English at the University of Iowa. A recipient of a NEA Fellowship and other recognitions, his work has appeared in numerous journals, magazines, and anthologies, including *Orion*, *Terrain.org*, *Fourth Genre*, and *The Best Spiritual Writing* series. He is the Regents/Foundation Distinguished Professor at the University of Nebraska at Omaha, where he directs the English Department's Creative Nonfiction Writing Program, and is a faculty member in the Goldstein Center for Human Rights. He lives with his family in the Loess Hills of western Iowa.

THE ICE CUBE PRESS began publishing in 1991 to focus on how to live with the natural world and to better understand how people can best live together in the communities they share and inhabit. Using the literary arts to explore life and experiences in the heartland of the United States we have been recognized by a number of well-known writers including: Bill Bradley, Gary Snyder, Gene Logsdon, Wes Jackson, Patricia Hampl, Greg Brown, Jim Harrison, Annie Dillard, Ken Burns, Roz Chast, Jane Hamilton, Daniel Menaker, Kathleen Norris, Janisse Ray, Craig Lesley, Alison Deming, Harriet Lerner, Richard Lynn Stegner, Richard Rhodes, Michael Pollan, David Abram, David Orr, and Barry Lopez. We've published a number of well-known authors including: Mary Swander, Jim Heynen, Mary Pipher, Bill Holm, Connie Mutel, John T. Price, Carol Bly, Marvin Bell, Debra Marquart, Ted Kooser, Stephanie Mills, Bill McKibben, Craig Lesley, Elizabeth McCracken, Derrick Jensen, Dean Bakopoulos, Rick Bass, Linda Hogan, Pam Houston, and Paul Gruchow. Check out Ice Cube Press books on our web site, join our email list, Facebook group, or follow us on Twitter. Visit booksellers, museum shops, or any place you can find good books and support true honest to goodness independent publishing projects so you can discover why we continue striving to "hear the other side."

Ice Cube Press, LLC (Est. 1991)
North Liberty, Iowa, Midwest, USA
Resting above the Silurian and Jordan aquifers
steve@icecubepress.com
Check us out on Twitter and Facebook
www.icecubepress.com
Subscribe to our substack *Ice Cube Press: Publishing, Writing, and Smart Life Secrets*

To Fenna Marie,
for which all the
trees I save & wish up on
are for you & your grins
may you keep *going, and going and going*...